JESUS AT CROSSROADS

ALI CHEGINI

(Messiah)

ALI CHEGINI

First edition self published in May 2020
Second edition self published in March 2022

All Scripture quotations, unless otherwise indicated, are taken from the Holy Bible, New International Version®, NIV®.
Copyright ©1973, 1978, 1984, 2011 by Biblica, Inc.™
Used by permission of Zondervan. All rights reserved worldwide.

The "NIV" and "New International Version" are trademarks registered in the United States Patent and Trademark Office by Biblica, Inc.™

Cover Art: Ali Chegini

Contents

Ghostly Boulevard	5
Silent Disillusion	9
More Questions	15
Leaving the Graveyard	19
The Unseen Realm	23
Whisper	29
In the Beginning Was the Word	35
Who Is God?	39
Catholic & Protestant	45
Jesus Is Not Reserved For Europeans	47
Look, I am Coming Soon!	51
My Baptism Ceremony	55
Comparison of Christianity & Islam	57

ALI CHEGINI

Ghostly Boulevard

Once upon a time, when darkness rose to chime, the bottom floor of hell was bluntly Iran, desolation and dread were publicly drawn. It was the year 2003, life was drear, empty of glee. I was studying in a spooky high school in the vicinity of a graveyard; the school that I named **Ghostly Boulevard**.

One dark downbeat day in Ghostly Boulevard, I decided to perform a harmless prank to energize the day. I thought it would be creative to keep the classroom's door blocked for a few minutes. I held the door knob passionately and did not let others come inside. It went on alright for a few minutes, but the situation escalated quickly. I heard a fierce knock; a mad voice was shouting; open the door! I recognized the voice; it was the savage schoolmaster whom I hated so much. He came in and attacked me viciously; he slapped me in the face repeatedly to the point that half of my face felt numb; I could hear a noise in my head sounding like a train whistle broadcasted directly into my skull. The whistle in my head began like a low-pitched noise; swiftly got louder and louder; sssssssssSSSSSSSSSSS! The noise dominated my skull rampantly to the point that I could not hear my surrounding environment anymore. I didn't know it back then, but years later, I found out those were signs of concussion.

What kind of animal slapp a teenager in the face like that?

A savage one indeed. I was only fifteen years old!

I casted long lasting bitter curse upon that heavy hand, O those damn headaches, and the hatred I built up toward the schoolmaster. I was cursing him everyday with much greed; a vicious savage animal indeed.

In those dark years, teachers in Iran were allowed to physically attack students without any further complications. It was considered part of the normal curriculum! Years later, when I was in Europe, I learned that if a teacher shows such violence in high school, he is seen as a criminal, and the act is seen as a serious crime.

That was not the only savage I had in my life; there were many wild beasts that I opted to delete. It was one thing when I was beaten up on the street, yet it was different when I experienced violence in school. The school that I hated so much, the school that I wished it was never built. I never understood why they'd built a school near a Muslim graveyard!

I was only fifteen years old, yet the pains in my life were much bigger than I could cope with.

By that age, I had been to graveyards many times. I experienced the Muslim burial, mourning and crying countless times; death and sorrow was a regular part of people's diet in Iran.

I remember being in the graveyard, with hundreds of dug graves ready to swallow dead bodies inside. Once, I layed down in one of those empty graves; wanting to know how it felt to go and never come back; It was a murky feeling indescribable in words; therefore I don't even try.

By that age, I was beaten up many times by many people; teachers, authority and many more. By that age, I felt I was born on the wrong side of the planet, at the wrong time. I just didn't know why the world around me was so wrecked and messed up. I developed a strong desire to curse those whom I hated, dozens of times per day; I cursed a lot of people in my childhood.

That year was critical in many ways. It was the same year that my views and attitude toward Islam was altered. I started thinking and asking questions about some of the widely accepted concepts in society, school, cultural and religious norms in Iran. A sequence of events led to a fundamental change in my worldview.

ALI CHEGINI

Silent Disillusion

Newborns in a Muslim country from Muslim parents were considered Muslim at birth; it was not a choice. Kids in Iran were taught to repeat verses of Quran and Arabic prayers at an early age, long before knowing what those verses meant.

The language of Iran is Persian[1]. Persian has almost the same alphabet as Arabic, however it is a completely different language; as a result, most Iranians don't understand Arabic at all.

Religious practices in my life started from an early age; by the time I was ten years old, I could already recite specific verses of the Quran. Between the ages of nine and fifteen, I used to go to mosque frequently to pray[2]; merely because I was brainwashed into thinking I would receive a tree in heaven every time I prayed in a mosque!

It was around the late 90s and the early 2000s in Iran; smart phones and high speed internet did not exist as it does nowadays. The era in which the flow of information was strictly tight, limited and censored to what the ruling authority would

---

[1] Persian language is also called Farsi
[2] Muslim prayer in Iran is called Namaz; in Arabic is called Salat

allow. The only available narrative was the one echoed through loud sound systems in mosques, courses in schools, state run TV and radio programs; no alternative narrative could be found.

I remember in those days, everytime I would turn on the TV, there was a Mullah[3] speaking about Islam, Quran, or some Islamic traditions. There were only 4 TV channels; most of the programs included one or more Mullahs. Occasionally there were programs to stream censored cartoons and football matches, but they were rare. Most programs were dominantly religious, filled with a sense of sorrow, mourning and crying; Islamic laments were dominantly spreading from every medium of broadcasting. There was not a single happy song coming out of the media, not the TV nor the radio; only sad marches, death chants, sorrow and sadness.

In Islamic cultures, people of high status, such as religious teachers and Mullahs, are determined as authorities. In such an environment, people ought to accept Islamic fundamentals with blind faith and never ask why.

As an adolescent living in a brainwashed society, I was faithfully following that model, the blind faith; I was a practicing Muslim up to a certain age; actively, engaged in daily prayers, reading Quran, fasting and following Allah. When I

---

[3] Mullah is also called Imam

was fifteen years old, while praying in a mosque, I questioned my own actions for the very first time. I started contemplating with myself during a daily prayer.

"Do you even know what you are repeating?" I asked myself.

"No, It's all Arabic; I don't get it."

"Why do you repeat verses if you don't understand their meaning?"

"I don't know; because I grew up thinking these are holy verses. I should just repeat them."

This happened to me multiple times until I finally decided to ask the questions from the Mullah who was leading the prayer in the mosque.

I asked the Mullah, "Why do we have to pray in Arabic?"

"Because Mohammad said Muslims should only pray in Arabic." He replied.

"Why can't we pray in Persian?"

"Because the Quran was written in Arabic, and Arabic is the only spoken language in heaven!"

I had a big problem with that answer; I fired a chain of nipping questions after hearing that.

"Does it mean in order to go to heaven one must speak Arabic?"

"Yes." He replied. I had a problem with that too.

"Isn't Allah the one who created the world and all the people, then why doesn't he let me pray in Persian?" I asked with a curious tone.

"Every religious practice must be done in Arabic ONLY to be accepted by Allah; the Quran came to Mohammad in Arabic and all the Muslims are obliged to pray ONLY in Arabic." He replied with an irritated tone.

This rang a bell in my mind; I didn't ask more questions; a dilemma was formed in my mind.

Could it be the Allah that I spent years worshiping, was actually an Arab god?

How come he'd only accept prayers in one language?

I was only fifteen years old, but at that age I was struggling to convince myself to stay a Muslim and continue worshiping Allah. I told myself, if Arabic is the only language spoken in Allah's heaven, I don't want to go to that heaven at all; I am not going to worship that god anymore.

I became disillusioned with Islam and I decided to leave my religion. A concrete opinion was formed in my mind.

Allah is Arab; therefore he belongs to Arabs, not to Persians.

That was a turning point in my life. I mentally left Allah. I stopped praying, fasting and reciting the Quran.

I became a silent observer with an agnostic worldview; I could not justify neither the belief that God exists, nor the belief that God does not exist. What I could justify was the fact that Allah is the god of Arabs, not the creator of the universe; I knew it well by that time, IF there was a creator, that couldn't be the Arab god.

In my mind, I established a baseline, a threshold to accept a creator. IF I would ever consider accepting a creator as God, that creator had to have certain minimal characteristics.

The creator had to be universal and not limited to the Arabian desert. The creator had to accept prayers in every language, not just in Arabic.

Living in a brainwashed society made me very hesitant about finding a creator; I was not sure if I could ever find one.

I never talked about holding an agnostic worldview with anyone. I was a quiet introvert and I didn't want to get beaten up. By that age, I was beaten up many times by many people; I knew how it felt. I was aware of the fact that in a Muslim environment, expressing such opinions would lead to complicated situations. I remained a silent observer and continued to pose questions instead of expressing my opinions.

Few months later, I decided to ask my teacher in school to explain the meaning behind some of the Quran's verses. The reaction I got from my teacher was murky!

More Questions

I had a few compulsory classes in high school such as Arabic language, Quran and Religion in Life. As these classes were part of the regular curriculum, I had to pass all these subjects to go to the next grade. These classes were like a playground for me to walk on the teacher's nerves. I always had a strong desire to ask questions, unlike other students in school, I would not care how the teacher would perceive my questions. As far as I was concerned, his job was to answer these questions; he was getting paid for it.

I was sixteen years old when I pulled out some verses from the Quran and decided to ask a couple of topics from the religious teacher in high school. One of the topics was about the story of a homosexual tribe called the Lut tribe; the other was a verse in Quran that I suspected it was about sexual exploitation of the women who were spoils of war.[4]

While the class was in session, I asked the teacher to explain the topics one by one and the meaning behind Allah's words. I explicitly asked him, which sin is the heaviest? Adultery

---
[4] Quran 4:24

between male and female or the homosexuality of the Loot tribe? I also asked him to translate the verse 4:24 in the Quran.

He got so mad at me for asking such relevant questions. I was not even criticizing the Quran, I was just asking him to clarify. He started shouting at me viciously. He humiliated me in front of other students and put many labels on me.

He shouted, "Aren't you ashamed of asking me such questions?"

I said, "Why should I be ashamed? It is the word of Allah, are you telling me Allah's words are immoral and shameful?"

That was like a bomb being dropped in the classroom; he got so angry and kicked me out of the classroom; I was sent to the principal's office; everyone in the administration office humiliated me; I was labeled as immoral and shameful. I carried a lot of labels during my school years in Ghostly Boulevard.

Time passed, I read more, and the issue crystallized more complications when I found out other verses in Quran and rules in Sharia law that allowed Muslim men to have a maximum of 4 permanent wives - with no limit on the temporary concubines! [5]

The same act that is considered adultery for a woman, punishable by worst type of death in Islam, is considered a right for a Muslim man!

---

[5] Quran 4:3

I investigated the issue further and found out Muslim nations of the world have always had many bloody disputes over different topics; but they all unanimously agree on this one core principle; the concept of having multiple wives, polygamy, is considered as a core fundamental Islamic belief. Indisputable and inseparable from Islam, widely practiced in almost all the Muslim countries of the world nowadays; countries such as Singapore, Iran, Saudi Arabia, United Arab Emirates, Qatar, Jordan, Indonesia, Bahrain, Pakistan, Iraq and many more.

I was deeply convinced that the Quran was not written for me, and Islam was not my religion. The more I found this kind of verses in Quran, I would become more confident that leaving Islam at age 15 was a good decision. Most of my schoolmates were not even thinking about these concepts at that age.

Years passed by, with much darkness in the sky. I graduated, without much honor, from Ghostly Boulevard; a few years later I came out of the graveyard.

ALI CHEGINI

Leaving the Graveyard

I was only twenty two, when I last saw the graveyard in dew. I left the graveyard and flew; I flew and flew, but never made it through. I did pass the seven seas, my path was far away from ease. I was adrift in Asia for many years, till I left the continent without much tears. I relocated to Denmark, where depression began to disembark.

When I was in my mid twenties, I received an offer letter from the Technical University of Denmark to enroll in a master's program in Computer Science & Engineering. I accepted the offer and became a student in one of the best universities in Europe.

Between the age of fifteen to thirty, I had lived my life holding an agnostic worldview. I could not justify neither the belief that God exists, nor the belief that God does not exist. The underlying issue with living such a life was the feeling of being separated from the world; being disconnected from the universe; not knowing who created all things; the earth, the clouds, the oceans, the galaxies, the stars and everything else could not come to existence spontaneously; somebody must have created everything, set the laws of the universe and let it run, but WHO did it and WHY?

For many years I tried to sort out these dilemmas in my mind relying on science and the answer scientists had; with the **Big Bang Model**.

Scientists could explain how the universe came to existence. Oversimply put, about 14 billion years ago, the entire universe and all specks of its energy was jammed into a very tiny point, a few millimeters. This extremely dense point then exploded with infinite force and propelled everything outwards and created billions of galaxies, including the one we live in.

What scientists could not answer was "**WHO** jammed all specks of energy into a very tiny point?"

Every explosion needs an initial trigger, it does not happen on it's own; what science couldn't answer was "**WHO** initiated the first trigger for the massive explosion?"

The climax of the dilemma was in the following question, "**WHY** was that jamming and the first explosion occurred?"

What was the **PURPOSE**?

In the best case scenario, science may be able to explain how the universe came to existence, but it doesn't explain why. One is the study of the **CAUSE**, and the other is the study of the **EFFECT**.

The path to search for life's meaning took me about 15 years to commute. I wanted to know why I came to this life. I wanted to know where I was going after this life. These questions and the fact that I was not able to answer them through the scientific lens, created an internal void, a vacuum, a black hole in me.

To fill the void, I would regularly go to bars and nightclubs; drank alcohol to forget the pain, but after a while I started to feel lonelier, frustrated and depressed. I learned that beer cans and tequila shots had limited shallow effect; they could defer the pain, but they could not eliminate it; the emptiness and the hopelessness would always come back; even more advanced, even more magnified. Alcohol could hide the problem under the surface for a short while, but it could never resolve it.

Who created all things, and **Why**?

I needed answers. I knew there was something missing in my life, I just didn't know what it was. I continued that lifestyle till the age of thirty.

One Sunday morning at a crossroads in Copenhagen, I heard something that I'd never heard before. I had no idea the course of my life was about to change forever.

The Unseen Realm

I spent 15 years of my life in a desolated state of mind; completely disconnected from the universe, not knowing if there was a God and if there was a divine power in motion.

Living in Denmark for a few years, broke me down into pieces and created a new version of me from scratch. After my graduation from the Technical University of Denmark in my late twenties, I went through a dark depressing period. This period of my life was the darkest and the loneliest time I ever had. I could rarely sleep at night and anxiety was a full time companion of mine. I distanced myself from everyone I knew in the school community; the void in me, the black hole, was getting deeper and deeper; it was eating me from inside.

It is kind of odd hearing on the news that Denmark is the happiest country on the planet. That statement might be true, but only for Danes; not for foreigners living in Denmark.

One of the unique characteristics of the Danes is that they value long term friendships, and if they know someone is there on a temporary basis, no one really has a tendency to form a relationship with that person. Most Danes have a couple of close friends from high school, they grow up together, go to university together, always keep their circle closed and reserved. If one has not gone to high school in Denmark, then there is very little chance he could form and maintain lasting friendships with Danes.

As an introvert, living in Denmark was enormously more difficult for me. I was stuck in a circle that I could not talk to anybody and nobody was talking to me. Not having friends and contacts with the outside world, made me feel more isolated and pushed me deeper down in the black hole; the pit of depression.

It can be quite hard for people to fathom the situation. How can someone live in the happiest country on the planet, but be depressed, lonely and frustrated?

Welcome to my old porch; a lonely attic without a torch; and very few sunny days. Not having enough sunlight exposure for almost nine months per year added to the depth of the black hole. Oh, I'd never forget those long Danish winters.

I felt completely disconnected from the universe and didn't have anybody to confabulate with. I was in a weak state of mind, utterly devastated. While I was struggling with my inner desolation in those dark days, I started contemplating about the meaning of life more. I wanted to find out if there was more to life than what I was experiencing. Many questions were roaring in my mind.

Is this life only limited to physical and material form?

Am I supposed to just get drowned in the ocean filled with darkness, depression, anxiety, emptiness, and loneliness?

Is there anyone who can rescue me?

Am I left alone in this world without a savior?

What's at the end of the story? What happens to me if I die tomorrow?

I struggled a lot with these questions; it never crossed my mind that the real problem was behind the scene; my lack of awareness about the unseen realm. It took me a lot of research to find out about the invisible side of my existence. When I read about the spirit, I could not promptly understand it. I had to read and reread a lot of material to be able to grasp just the tip of the iceberg.

Simply and condensely put, I found out as human beings we are a composite of body, mind and spirit. We have a physical body equipped with sensory factors that can see, touch, hear, smell and taste; we also have an intellectual mind that can think, reason and make decisions based on input the sensory factors provide; yet at the same time we have an invisible spiritual side that most of us don't pay any attention to. The spiritual side of us lives in a different dimension, in the unseen realm.

While contemplating about this, I realized many of the scenes I could recall from my dreams and nightmares, did not have a physical replica in the visible world. This made me ponder about the idea that in addition to the visible dimension, there must be another invisible dimension to life; a dimension that I was unaware of; a dimension that I could not access through my physical body, but I could no longer dismiss.

I knew about the physical body and the mind, but never knew about the spirit. For so long, I'd always tried to live and sort everything out relying on my body and mind, while completely ignoring the spiritual dimension. My struggles and inner turmoil had led me on a path to study my own essence, my own existence on a deeper level.

For so long, I was trying to find something on the outside to feel better, but I realized whatever I needed was already in me. I understood that I should not seek fulfillment on the outside. I realized that I have a spirit, the soul, which is invisible, but I didn't know how to connect with it. I didn't know how it could change my life.

While studying and researching my own essence, I came across a profound idea; that in order to get healed in my physical life, I should first get healed in my spirit. I was unaware of my spiritual side for my entire life, but when I studied my own essence, I became eager to find out how I could get healed in my spirit.

I studied the law of vibration; which elaborates everything vibrates on a specific frequency; nothing rests; we are living in the ocean of motions.

As Albert Einstein said, "**Everything in Life is Vibration.**"

Simply put, if we take an ice cube and look at it under a microscope, we can see every molecule vibrating on a low frequency; if we add heat to the ice cube, it will melt and transforms into liquid form which vibrates on a higher frequency; if we add more heat to the liquid water, it will turn into steam which vibrates on a much higher frequency; they are still the same molecules, but in each form they vibrate on a specific frequency and they don't look the same.

I discovered that at any given time, the body vibrates on a specific frequency; the mind vibrates on a unique frequency, so does the spirit. I found out that in order to feel wholeness I must tune into the right frequencies; body, mind and spirit, they all have to be tuned into the right frequency. It's not enough to fix one; all three have to be tuned and balanced.

I could understand how to change the frequency of my mind through positive thinking; I could understand how to have the right frequency in my body through a healthy diet; however I was having a hard time understanding the spiritual frequency, how it worked and how to tune it to the right frequency.

I discovered that when body, mind and spirit lose a harmonious relationship, that creates disease, depression, anxiety and more issues. It occured to me that the missing link was the lack of awareness about my own spirit. I had to open my mind to understand the spirit.

It was uncomfortable trying to grasp a concept that was foreign to me for my entire life. One day something happened at a crossroads in Copenhagen that changed my perspective.

Whisper

Living in Europe changed me a lot, but I never gave up my food preferences. There was a neighborhood in Copenhagen called Nørrebro; I used to go there frequently, because there were many Middle Eastern restaurants in the area and I always prefered Middle Eastren food.

The area had always been a paradoxical neighborhood. It had a high density of Muslim population, a crossroads with a big mosque on one side, and a pentecostal church on the opposite side. Many of the shootings and violent incidents in Copenhagen used to happen in this neighborhood.

I knew about the church, Copenhagen Christian Center, because one of my friends from engineering school used to play guitar in the church.

I knew about the mosque because it had my name on it; Imam Ali mosque!

One Sunday morning, in mid April 2019, I finished eating food in a restaurant; I was walking in the neighborhood, not knowing my life was about to change forever.

I was passing by feeling anxious and depressed, not knowing where I was going. I reached the busy crossroads, then I heard something; a whisper that I alone could hear.

"Come to Church, You are invited. Come to Church, You will feel better! Come to Church, I will make you!"

I was deeply impacted, confused and puzzled. It was not a natural feeling; it was supernatural. It was not happening in the physical realm. There were many people at the crossroads, but they could not hear what I could hear.

They were simply passing by, through the crossroads impossible to untie. I was the only one feeling mesmerized, utterly cracked and surprised.

Till that day, I never had such a vivid supernatural experience. What was that? Come to Church, You are invited!

I pondered with myself for a few moments. I knew there was a church nearby; the whisper invited me to go there.

I asked myself, why shouldn't I go?

What is the worst that can happen?

They might say you are not a Christian, you can't come in.

I was fine with that. I decided to go to church.

I arrived at the church's front door. A Danish girl welcomed me and shook my hand. That was kind of odd, because Danes don't usually shake hands with someone they don't know;

especially if that someone is not blond! I was glad by the warm welcome and went inside. The service had just started a few moments before my arrival. When I walked into the entrance door of the main hall, a middle aged Danish guy was standing in front of the door.

He came to me and said, "Hi, how are you doing today? I have never met you in the church before. What is your name? Where are you from?"

I said, "My name is Ali, I am from Iran. It's my first time in the church."

He said, "Welcome. My name is Palle and I am a pastor in this church."

He invited me in, and helped me to find a seat. He said, "Ali, this is so strange. We have a special guest today; a Turkish pastor who flew from Turkey to preach a sermon here; and he was praying on the stage a few moments ago." that, "Lord bring more people from the Middle East and Muslim background to Jesus; that is the only way to change the world."

That was indeed very strange. I asked myself, "Was that just a coincidence?"

"How come I never heard such a whisper before? And today at the same time a special guest was praying, I heard a voice that took me to church!"

I couldn't call that just a coincidence.

I was thrilled to have a chance to watch a Christian service. The service started. Two pastors were on stage, one was preaching in Danish, the other was translating to English. I could easily follow the message. Time passed and they started worshiping with music. I never knew how Danes worship.

It was an amazing experience. There was a complete music band on stage with multiple instruments such as drums, guitar, bass, keyboard, etc. Combination of 3 singers on stage with amazing voices and a choir group created an extraordinary atmosphere. It was indeed an uplifting and energetic experience; moments I never had before.

I was extremely fascinated as I always had a huge passion for music and instruments. Being a musician myself, I could feel the dopamine rush just by looking at a musical instrument. I felt much better. I started to appreciate what the whisperer was telling me. **Come to Church, you will feel better!** I realized there was a supernatural force that brought me to that place, to that moment, and there was a purpose for everything.

The Christian worship was the exact opposite of what I could remember from worshiping Allah in mosques! When I was a Muslim living in Iran 15 year prior, people would only go to mosque for funeral, to cry and mourn. No one was ever allowed to bring a guitar inside a mosque. Playing this type of music in a mosque would produce a direct ticket to hell; it was strictly forbidden. Mosque had always been resembling death, sorrow, tears and sadness; the mosque was never a place to feel happy nor uplifted.

Many questions were roaring in my mind while listening to worship songs. The service reached a point when it was time for prayers. Pastors lined up against a specific wall; people could go to them and ask for prayers. I went to Palle, the pastor I met at the front door.

I asked him to pray for me so I can cope with the dreadful feeling of void, anxiety and depression. He prayed; while he was praying I felt such a peaceful moment; just as if a stormy ocean in my heart suddenly calmed down and my mind started vibrating on a different frequency. In that moment of prayer, I was certain about one thing; I will definitely come back to this place again.

When he finished praying, he asked, "Would you like to come back to the church again?"

I instantly responded with a firm yes. I had a lot of questions about the Christian God, Jesus, and the Bible. I wanted to find out the truth.

Who was Jesus?

What did he do during his life?

What happened to him?

What does the Bible say about spirit?

Did Jesus mention the unseen realm?

Did Jesus answer the Question, "Why was this universe created?"

Did Jesus answer the Question, "Who created the universe?" And many more questions.

Before the end of the service, pastors said on the stage "If there is somebody new, raise your hand to receive a gift." I raised my hand, and received the gift which was an English Bible; the New International Version[6] published by Zondervan.

After the service, I set an appointment with the pastor to meet in the church a few days later. That was a great chance to ask my questions; I was keen to deeply investigate Jesus and the Chrsitian faith.

Meanwhile I decided to read the Bible to see if I could find comforting words; to see if I could communicate with the words. I had no idea that the most liberating journey of my life was about to get started.

---

[6] New International Version is abbreviated as NIV

In the Beginning Was the Word

After my first day in Copenhagen Christian Center, I started reading the Bible frequently. As I was never exposed to Christian material by that age, I was very excited to have a Bible. The good news was that I could easily understand the text in the Bible; simple plain English translation that required no help to interpret it. I was so thrilled to see the Bible was not written in Arabic!

There was something special about this book. Every time I was anxious and uneasy, reading the Bible would calm me down and put me in a different state of mind. Almost as if a stormy ocean in my essence gradually calms down.

I started with the New Testament. I opened a random page, it was the book of Mark, chapter 2. I started reading verses 13 to 17. It was a story about Jesus having dinner with sinners and tax collectors. On seeing this, teachers of the Jewish law, the Pharisees, asked the disciples: "Why does he eat with tax collectors and sinners?"

On hearing this, Jesus said, **"It is not the healthy who need a doctor, but the sick. I have not come to call the righteous, but sinners."** [7]

I was amazed with such a kind and unique response. Jesus would not see himself as a highly exalted person who should avoid socializing with sinners in order to keep his image in the society untainted. He was willing to take the risk to be ostracized by the religious leaders, just to be kind with sinners and outcasts. This meant If Jesus was here in my time, he would have dinner with me; even though I was an unbeliever, a doubter, an agnostic for a long time.

I continued reading the New Testament and I was quickly lost in the pages. The more I read, the more it captured my heart. The first page of the book of John blew my mind; a page highly potent and beautifully compressed, profoundly complex, yet simply expressed. The page that answered one of my fundamental questions; yet crystalized more questions!

"In the Beginning was the Word, and the Word was with God, and the Word was God. He was with God in the beginning. Through him all things were made; without him nothing was made that has been made." [8]

---

[7] Mark 2:17, NIV
[8] John 1:1-3

These verses had neatly condensed an answer to the question: "**WHO** created all things?" Yet, they produced new questions in my mind.

How could this be?

How could the Word be with God, and be God simultaneously?

Then I read, **"THE WORD BECAME FLESH AND MADE HIS DWELLING AMONG US. WE HAVE SEEN HIS GLORY, THE GLORY OF THE ONE AND ONLY SON, WHO CAME FROM THE FATHER, FULL OF GRACE AND TRUTH."** [9]

At first encounter, this verse sounded so complex, so profound, and difficult to process. I could never imagine a life in which the creator of the universe comes down and lives among people. Wow!

I had to pause for a while, as my mind could not compile. I could not process this masterpiece, yet my heart began to boil piece by piece.

I flipped to the very beginning of the Old Testament, the first page of the book of Genesis. "In the beginning God created the heavens and the earth. Now the earth was formless and

---

[9] John 1:14

empty, darkness was over the surface of the deep, and the Spirit of God was hovering over the waters." [10]

There it was again; same answer to the question: "**WHO created all things?**" Yet, these verses produced another question in my mind.

How could the Spirit of God be hovering over the waters?

I had never read such a stimulating book in my life. I enjoyed reading the Bible more than any other book. By the time I closed the Bible, I knew I was going to keep this book forever; whatever I might lose, I would never lose my Bible. Gradually, I turned reading the Bible into a daily habit.

I had many questions, and I was eagerly waiting for my appointment with Palle, the Danish pastor, in the church.

---

[10] Genesis 1:1-2

Who Is God?

I went to church again for my appointment with pastor Palle. The church was empty and quiet. We sat down in his office and started talking.

I had a deep longing to find out who the Christian God is. I knew Christians believe in the Trinity, the concept of Triune God, but I did not know what it meant. I asked Palle about Trinity. He explained it as simply as he could. I condensed what I understood from his explanations.

In Christian doctrine, Trinity defines God as one being consisting of three persons. Christians believe there is only **One God**, who exists in **Three persons**.

The first person of Trinity is **God the Father** who controls the universe and created everything from scratch; heaven and earth, Adam and Eve, Angles, light and everything we can possibly think of.

The second person of Trinity is **God the Son**, Jesus Christ. God the Father sent his only begotten Son to earth to be the ultimate way of salvation for humanity. He sent his own Son to live among people in order to suffer the same pain we suffer, feel the same hunger and thirst we feel, get betrayed like we get betrayed, experience torture and be crucified. God wanted to experience all the human feelings deeply and show that He can conquer death.

The third person of Trinity is **God the Holy Spirit**; the gift one can receive after accepting Jesus Christ in heart; believing He was the only begotten Son of God, who was crucified on the cross, and was resurrected on the third day. Through this gift, anyone can have direct intimate access to the Father. Anyone who receives the Holy Spirit becomes a child of the Most High God.

Time for the meeting was up, and I left the church with a seed in my mind. I was deeply fascinated by the words; the heaviest concepts I ever heard in my life. The idea that I could have direct intimate access to the creator was like a seed of hope planted in my mind; the mind that was aching filled with discomfort; aching like a caterpillar in the middle of metamorphosis, right before it turns into a butterfly.

On first hearing, things did not click in my mind right away. I still had two profound questions.

How could one God exist in three persons simultaneously?

In a nutshell, is there ONE God or THREE?

I wanted to study the Christian God, the Trinity deeper. I had a feeling this would be the most important research of my life. I dedicated some quality time to contemplate on what I learned from Palle, and to investigate the topic on my own. After reading a considerable amount of related material online and offline, I was able to grasp the concept of the Triune God. I believe the best way to explain the concept is by using a couple of familiar analogies.

The simplest analogy I use to explain the Trinity is by correlating God with half a liter box of ice cream that has banana chocolate flavor.

It is ONE box of ice cream considered as ONE unit, but when you eat it, you sense multiple tastes in your mouth. It is ONE ice cream which provides multiple flavors in your mouth simultaneously; you can taste the banana flavor, chocolate flavor and milky flavor, all at the same time. ONE unit with THREE different personalities; a banana personality, a chocolate personality, a milky personality all together form ONE Being. It is ONE in THREE.

A more sophisticated analogy I use to explain Trinity is by correlating God's nature with an atom.

ONE atom consists of THREE types of particle; protons, neutrons and electrons. It is ONE atom with THREE different personalities simultaneously. It is ONE in THREE. If you observe any of the atomic particles at a given time, for instance the proton, you can realize that while it is a particle with its unique nature as a proton, it is also an essence of the atom. It is the proton, yet it is part of the atom at the same time.

After I could understand and explain the Trinity using these analogies, something else clicked in my mind. I remembered my own existence; I remembered I have a body, mind and spirit. I am ONE being, who consists of THREE parts.

I realized, if many things in nature including myself can be ONE in THREE, then God can also be ONE in THREE.

By realizing that, my analytical mind was able to connect the dots and process the question: "How could the Word be with God, and be God simultaneously?"

THE WORD BECAME FLESH

In the Beginning was the Word, and the **Word was with God**, and the **Word was God**.

I realized that Jesus is the Word who became flesh; as a person of the Trinity, Jesus, is one essence of God; almost the same way a proton is an essence of one atom.

This rang a bell in my mind; things clicked. In the beginning **Jesus was with God**, and **Jesus was God**; almost the same way a **proton is with the atom**, and **it is part of the atom**.

After my mind connected the dots and could process two persons of the Trinity, God the Father, and God the Son, I was utterly astonished by thinking about the third person of Trinity; God the Holy Spirit.

For a long time, I was struggling to grasp the spirit. I was puzzled about the unseen realm; the invisible side, the spiritual dimension. I found out the Bible had mentioned spirit over 500 times from Genesis to Revelation. I could not overlook dozens of verses in the Bible stating the importance of spirit in life. I read in the Gospel of John when Jesus said, "But the Advocate, the Holy Spirit, whom the Father will send in my name, will teach you all things and will remind you of everything I have said to you." [11]

There it was; answer to my other question: "How could the Spirit of God be hovering over the waters?"

The Spirit of God could hover over the waters just like electrons in an atom hovering around the protons and neutrons.

The Trinity, the Triune God, had existed from the beginning.

The notion that I could receive a part of God, the Holy Spirit, to dwell in me was so comforting, so enlightening, so illuminating.

---

[11] John 14:26

It took me a long time to realize that my spirit was like a boat drifting in the dark ocean of life without a destination, devastated and lost; that my spirit was vibrating on a wrong frequency, out of harmony with the divine nature of God.

I was delighted when I found out through Jesus Christ, I could receive the third person of the Trinity, God the Holy Spirit.

My mind was blown away when I tried to imagine having direct intimate access to the infinite source of energy and Love, the universal God who created all things, the creator who initiated the first trigger for the Big Bang! Direct intimate access from my own Spirit to the Spirit of God that was hovering over the waters at the beginning!

Catholic & Protestant

Next time I met Palle in the church, I asked him about differences between Catholic and Protestant views. I had heard the names before, but I never knew how they differed from each other. I condensed my understanding from his explanations and my own research.

I inferred that Catholics and Protestants share the same beliefs about Jesus. They both believe Jesus lived, was crucified and was resurrected on the third day. They both believe communion and baptism are very important.

One of the core differences is about the authority to forgive the sins. Catholic beliefs indicate that the Pope and saints have authority to forgive the sins, however in Protestant's belief it is only God who has authority to forgive the sins; not the priests, not the Pope, not the saints; the one and only God who has sent his own Son and sacrificed him on the cross to pay the penalty for all sinners.

Protestants believe salvation is a free gift of God and you can not earn it. The price for all sins is already paid through Jesus' blood; you don't earn your salvation, but you receive it by grace and mercy. Jesus' blood saves you by grace and mercy. In contrast, Catholics believe Jesus offers salvation only to those who work for it; something that must be earned; you must follow certain disciplines and practices to earn it.

Another difference is about purgatory, the concept which Catholics regard as a place for cleansing and preparation for heaven. In Protestnat beliefs purgatory does not exist; a believer in Christ will directly go to heaven without a need to be cleansed in purgatory.

There is much more to write about this topic; a topic that can be a book on its own, but the aforementioned important aspects were enough for me to lean toward the Protestant beliefs. Protestant's vision resonated with me deeply and I could relate with it better. I never doubted choosing between Catholic beliefs and Protestant beliefs.

Reaching to that stage, the dominant question in my mind was about Jesus' blood. How could Jesus' blood wash away all sins?

Jesus Is Not Reserved For Europeans

Many of the concepts I learned about Christianity in Denmark were contrary to what I used to believe. In middle school and high school in Iran, religious teachers had injected the beliefs in my mind that Jesus is not for the people of the Middle East; that Christianity is the religion of the West.

What I heard in the church in Denmark was so profound, so different, so fresh; ideas that were like fresh seeds of hope planted in my mind.

Anyone can have a relationship with God, regardless of their sins in the past, their language, previous beliefs, skin color, nationality, hair color, and eye color. Anyone can be adopted to God's family through Jesus Christ. Anyone can become a child of the Most High God. The price for all sins is already paid on the cross by Jesus' blood.

The more I read the Bible, the more I felt Jesus. I could feel the fresh seeds sprouting in my mind; sprouts that breathed a refreshing air in my mind; a refreshing air with a profound message; **Jesus is not reserved for Europeans and the West! Jesus is for everyone. Jesus is universal.**

A sequence of events started to flash back in my mind. I heard the whisper and went to church; then the storm in my heart calmed down in prayer; then I read that unique story in the Bible about Jesus having dinner with sinners and outcasts; subsequently learning that Jesus wants to save me by absolute grace and mercy, with unconditional love; realizing the fact that by saying yes to Jesus I can become a child of the Most High God.

I could feel heavy chains from the past beliefs getting loose in my mind; feelings that I can only describe as metamorphosis in my mind.

Many Christian concepts became clear by that stage, but I still wanted to dig deeper into salvation. I had a few more fundamental questions left.

How could Jesus' blood save me and pay for my sins?

Why was Jesus' blood so special?

I investigated salvation further and what I discovered was phenomenal, so heavy, so profound.

To grasp the concept of salvation, it is essential to recall the Trinity; **ONE** God in **THREE** persons. Briefly put, in Christian doctrine, Jesus himself is one essence of God, a part of God. Considering this important aspect, the best way I could understand salvation was by associating it with the following analogy.

If a son stole some valuables from his father's jewelry store, then came to his father confessing and asking for forgiveness, the father has the right to forgive him; however the accounts haven't been balanced. Someone has to pay for the stolen valuables; if the father desires, he can pay for his son's debt from his own wealth.

In this analogy, we are the son; the father is God. We incurred a debt against God, because we all have sinned; the price of our sins is death. God sacrificed part of his own essence, Jesus Christ, on the cross to pay the penalty for our sins; balancing the accounts with his blood. Jesus is God in human form, and if God decides to pay for the sins with his blood, no one can stop him. He is the creator and the owner of the universe. Jesus' blood is special, because it is God's blood.

An essence of God, his only begotten Son, was crucified on the cross with the most painful death; his blood was shed to save all sinners; to give the chosen ones a new breath.

I read in the Gospel of Matthew, **"No one knows the Son except the Father, and no one knows the Father except the Son and those to whom the Son chooses to reveal him."** [12]

---

[12] Matthew 11:27

Salvation clicked and when it did, I had to cope with the fact I went through life for thirty years without being exposed to these concepts. The fact dawned on me that I lost many years of my life, living lonely and frustrated, not knowing I could be connected to God, just because I was born on the wrong side of the planet!

Then I asked myself, "Am I among those to whom Jesus chooses to reveal God?"

Look, I am Coming Soon!

What I had read in the Bible about Jesus having dinner with sinners was being echoed in my head like a stereo. **"It is not the healthy who need a doctor, but the sick. I have not come to call the righteous but sinners."**

I read in another verse where Jesus said, **"I am the way and the truth and the life. No one comes to the Father except through me."** [13]

Then I found the message I needed so much in the midst of depression and anxiety.

"Come to me, all you who are weary and burdened, and I will give you rest. Take my yoke upon you and learn from me, for I am gentle and humble in heart, and you will find rest for your souls. For my yoke is easy and my burden is light." [14]

As I was eager to find out about the final destiny, I turned to the last page of the Bible in the book of Revelation; the climax of my search for meaning.

---

[13] John 14:6
[14] Matthew 11:28-30

"Look, I am coming soon! My reward is with me, and I will give to each person according to what they have done. I am the Alpha and the Omega, the First and the Last, the Beginning and the End." [15]

After much research, contemplating and soul-searching in the midst of depression, I finally arrived at the conclusion that God exists; that God created me because He desired to be in a relationship with me; that God loves me; that God wants me to know him personally and intimately. God does not want to be an abstract idea in my mind, but He wants to live in a temple deep in my heart. God wants to save me and He said if I have faith as small as a mustard seed, I will be saved. He wants to save me by grace and mercy through His only begotten Son, Jesus Christ. The loving God who will give me the free gift of salvation; the loving God who created the universe; who wants to adopt me as His child; the heavenly Father that will give me an eternal life in heaven when my time on earth is over. I don't even have to earn my ticket to heaven; He will give me the ticket by His infinite grace and mercy.

I felt I was ready to make the most important decision of my life; I was ready to let Jesus come in and accept him in my heart.

---

[15] Revelation 22:12-13

I decided to say yes to Jesus in the church and have my pastor praying for me in my new path.

Eventually, by the end of April 2019, I said yes to Jesus and made the declaration in Copenhagen Christian Center.

Heavenly Father, I thank you for sending your only begotten Son to save me. I thank you that by sacrificing your only Son you paid the price for all my sins; your blood was shed on the cross, so I can have a new life. I now believe in your Son, Jesus Christ, and accept him in my heart, as my Lord and my Savior. Amen.

ALI CHEGINI

My Baptism Ceremony

One Sunday morning in the church, they announced there would be an upcoming baptism ceremony in Mid June 2019. I was eager to learn about baptism and its importance in Christian faith. I found a few verses in the Bible about the time when Jesus was baptized.

Jesus came to the Jordan river to be baptized by John the baptist. John said to Jesus, "I need to be baptized by you, and do you come to me?" Jesus replied, "Let it be so now; it is proper for us to do this to fulfill all righteousness." [16]

I read another verse about acknowledging Jesus in public. Jesus said, "I tell you, whoever publicly acknowledges me before others, the Son of Man will also acknowledge before the angels of God." [17]

I read another verse about being born in water and spirit. Jesus said, "Very truly I tell you, no one can enter the kingdom of God unless they are born of water and the Spirit." [18]

---

[16] Matthew 3:14-15
[17] Luke 12:8
[18] John 3:5

Knowing the fact that Jesus himself was baptized, I was certain I wanted to get baptized. I realized baptism was a very important step to complete my transition to a new life; a new life starting from scratch in the name of Jesus. I understood at the moment of being baptized, my old life would end and my new life would begin.

Eventually, on 16 June 2019, I was baptized in a public ceremony in Copenhagen Christian Center. I'd never forget that day; the best day of my life. Hundreds of believers were in the auditorium praying for me at the moment of regeneration; cheering and clapping when they heard my declaration on stage. Pastor Palle baptized me in the name of Jesus Christ.

He told me a couple of interesting facts after the ceremony; that I was the very first person from Muslim background to ever get baptised in that church in Denmark; that I was the very first person that he ever baptised from the Middle East.

What an amazing day it was. The best day of my life.

About a month after my baptism ceremony I relocated to a new country. My life in the new country has been so hectic like a roller coaster ride, with corona pandemic on the side; so immense that it is a book on its own; a book that I may write one day.

Comparison of Christianity & Islam

When it comes to comparing Christianity and Islam, there are many books out there, however most of the authors have not been a serious follower of both religions in one lifetime. They were either born in Christian environment, grew up in church for their entire life, then wrote a perspective from that lens; or they were born in Muslim environment, went to mosque for their entire life, then wrote a perspective from that lens. While those perspectives are both valuable and needed to grasp each school of thought deeper, I believe there is also an immense need for more books to be written by authors who have lived both lives; life of a Muslim and life of a Christian.

A book written from a convert's perspective can provide a unique opportunity to readers by allowing them to look at the purpose of life from two different lenses simultaneously. Contemplating about THE REAL GOD is so profound and complex, that without having both lenses, one can easily end up in a deep ditch; not knowing THE REAL GOD will surely lead to the gates of Hades.

I like this one liner which reads, "Walk a mile in my shoes before you judge me." I walked miles in both shoes; Muslim shoes and Christian shoes. In this chapter I condensed my findings and perspective about THE REAL GOD.

In order to investigate differences between Christianity and Islam, the core building blocks of these two faiths must be observed under historical microscope. While this chapter is not an exhaustive comparison between the two faiths, in my view, it is adequate to illuminate the borders and distinguish the irreconcilable differences.

The most important pillar in Christianity is Jesus and the most important pillar in Islam is Mohammad. I was shocked and astonished by what I found out about these two important figures after investigating the earliest and the most trustworthy records written about their lives.

Regarding the life of Jesus, everything can be found in the Bible; however regarding the life of Mohammad very little can be found in the Quran; to investigate his life, one must refer to books of hadiths, the only available records written about his life.

About Mohammad

Earlier in the book I discussed one of the inseparable, indisputable core foundation of Islam which is polygamy. To state the fact explicitly, Islam allows Muslim men to have maximum of four wives simultaneously, but Mohammad himself had at least seven wives at some point during his lifetime.

According to many Islamic sources, Mohammad married Aisha when she was only 6 years old; that marriage was consummated three years later when she was 9 and Mohammad was 52 years old! [19]

The name Aisha is immensely loved and respected by many Muslim families around the world to the extent that they still name their newborn daughters Aisha; to honor and resemble the name of the youngest Mohammad's wives.

An objective observer can relate the following fact to the example Mohammad set for his followers by his actions; having a child bride is still widely practiced nowadays in many Muslim regions of the world; too many young girls in Muslim world are being forced to get married at such an early age which is very harmful for their health.

---

[19] Sahih Bukhari 7.62.64; 7.62.65; 7.62.88; Sahih Muslim 8.3310; 8.3311.

Polygamy and child bride at one side of the narrative, another side is painted with blood and beheadings. It is written in Islamic sources that he led an attack on unarmed Jews.[20] In the battle of the Trench, the Jewish tribe of Qurayza was defeated and slaughtered by Mohammad and his army; in that single battle, they captured and beheaded more than 500 men and teenage boys. After the men were killed, they sold the woman and children into slavery and distributed their possessions among themselves. [21]

Multiple reputable sources recorded that Mohammad told people to drink camel's urine[22]; a tradition which is still being practiced nowadays in parts of the Middle East!

Such accounts are numerous and endless. Most Muslims have not heard these narratives; they have only heard a filtered version of the truth about Mohammad and his life.

I was born in a Muslim country and I was not aware of these narratives when I was a Muslim. It was only when I had access to uncensored content that I found out about such narratives.

To sum up this section, I mention a shaking statistic about the number of battles, raids and military operations Mohammad

---

[20] Sahih Bukhari 1.11.584.
[21] Guillaume, *Life of Muhammad*, 464.
[22] Sahih Bukhari 8.82.794; Sahih Muslim 16.4130.

was involved in. According to Islamic sources he commissioned or participated in more than **60** battles, raids and military conflicts combined, full of bloodshed, in a span of **9 years**!

Numerous beheadings and bloodshed occured in those battles; any nations or tribes which opposed Muslims were either forced to convert to Islam, or killed.

It was heartbreaking when my mind connected the dots from Persian history to Islam. At least in one of the aforementioned battles, Persia was defeated; all the horrible scenes that I read about, had occurred in Persia.

It was heartbreaking to realize that 1400 years ago Persia was conquered by Mohammad and his army, the entire population were forced to convert to Islam by the sword; many were killed and few escaped. 1400 years later, 96 percent of the population in Iran are still Muslim!

About Jesus, the God in human form

When I studied the life of Jesus Christ I was amazed. I could not find any bloodshed or war caused by Him. Jesus was the exact opposite of Mohammad.

Jesus never triggered any war; never led an army; never advocated for violence; never had a child bride; never forced anybody to convert to Christianity; never beheaded any of his enemies.

Even when the issue was about self defense, He did not allow violence. His message was always about peace and love. When a large crowd armed with swords and clubs came to arrest Him, one of his companions reached for his sword, drew it out and struck the servant of the high priest. Jesus said, Put your sword back in its place, for all who draw the sword will die by the sword. [23]

When Jesus conquered death and was risen on the third day, He did not take revenge; He broadcasted the message of love, forgiveness, and peace; even toward those who crucified him! He forgave everyone who believed in him, and those who didn't believe were left unharmed.

---

[23] Mathew 26:52

Jesus offered the free gift of salvation to all who loved the LORD and accepted him as the Savior; never by force but only by grace and mercy.

He was kind to Jews and Gentiles without blaming them for who they are. His teaching, way of life, and actions had always been centered around mercy, love, compassion, forgiveness and kindness.

There are numerous prophecies about the coming of the Savior in the Bible. The one I like so much is from the Eagle eye prophet Isaiah. About 700 years before Jesus' birth, Isaiah prophesied his birth. "Therefore the Lord himself will give you a sign: The virgin will conceive and give birth to a son, and will call him Immanuel."[24] Immanuel means God with us.

The Gospel of Matthew reminisces the fulfillment of scripture through the person of Jesus Christ.[25]

---

[24] Isaiah 7:14
[25] Matthew 1:18-23

Epilogue

Comparing the actions of Jesus Christ and Mohammad was an illuminating step for me. I understood that each tree is recognized by its own fruit. There is a path leading to light and there is a path leading to darkness; these two paths do not end up in the same place.

Aside from the actions of Jesus and Mohammad, I found other profound fundamental differences between the two faiths.

The Muslim god never promised to come down to earth and dwell among the followers; the Muslim god never promised presence, but only a paradise; even that paradise had never been guaranteed; a Muslim believer may get there after performing the so-called good deeds like Jihad, killing non Muslims and etc. The concept of salvation does not exist in Islam.

This is in absolute contrast to Christianity. The Christian God, which I found to be the only TRUE GOD, had promised presence; He promised to dwell among the believers; He did come down to earth; He did live among the people; He did experience all the human sufferings; He did die on the cross to pay the penalty for the sins of all. He did conquer death; He had risen on the third day; He did promise to come back again to create a new heaven and a new earth.

I see salvation as a core fundamental difference between the two faiths; In Jesus Christ, salvation is guaranteed not through the so-called deeds, but by the infinite grace and mercy; unconditional love that surpasses understanding.

I was astonished when I read God's promise to dwell among the believers in Christ. In the book of Revelation, I read "And I heard a loud voice from the throne saying, **"Look! God's dwelling place is now among the people, and he will dwell with them. They will be his people, and God himself will be with them and be their God."** [26]

Christ did not come to give us religion; He came to give us relationship. Relationship with the creator who walks with us, who talks with us, holds us in His arms and carries us on wings like an eagle. Jesus came to provide direct intimate access to the Father.

When the tunnel of my life was drowned in the darkness, I found only one light; the one and only light is my Lord Jesus Christ. As Christ forgave me, I forgave those who have wronged me in the past. Those that I wrote about them in this book, and many that I chose to delete; I forgave them all in the name of Jesus Christ.

---

[26] Revelation 21:3

I read in the Bible, Abraham was 75 years old and childless, when God promised him a miracle, a son from Sarah in that old age. Abraham was 100 years old, and Sarah was 90 years old when the promised child was born. It took 25 years for the promise of God to come to pass, but it did come to pass.

I have learnt from the Bible that when I pray, God packs the answer to my prayer and ships the package to the FAITH STREET. He just doesn't say when the package will arrive. It will arrive on his timeline.

God said, **"Ask and it will be given to you; seek and you will find; knock and the door will be opened to you."** [27]

I asked God for many miracles; some have already come to pass, and some not yet. I praise the Lord for those that have already come to pass and I praise the Lord for those that are on the way.

At the time of writing this book, the ghost of depression and lack has not yet fully left me, but I have a mustard seed faith that it will eventually leave, in the name of Jesus.

I believe and declare that the promises of healing and abundant life will come to pass. I will wait on the Lord patiently, as long as it takes.

---

[27] Matthew 7:7

I am not yet ready to come out of my shell. I am not yet what I need to be, but I thank God I am not what I used to be. I am not yet where I need to be, but I thank God I am not where I used to be.

"Yet you, Lord, are our Father.

    We are the clay, you are the potter;

    We are all the work of your hand." [28]

When I was at the most important crossroads of my life, I gave my life to Christ. By writing this book, I long to preach the good news about the Lord, the only Savior who can save all sinners.

You might be facing your crossroads in life; I long to share the good news with you; **THE RAINBOW IS ON THE WAY.** God said, "I have set my rainbow in the clouds, and it will be the sign of the covenant between me and the earth. Whenever I bring clouds over the earth and the rainbow appears in the clouds, I will remember my covenant between me and you and all living creatures of every kind." [29]

In all my imperfections, as the least in THE KINGDOM OF GOD, I tried to express what I learned about the Lord as condensed as possible, in less than 12,000 words.

---

[28] Isaiah 64:8
[29] Genesis 9:13-15

I wish to invite you to think about the TRUE GOD, why He created you, and what He wants from you.

Finally, I long to tell you that God said, **"Enter through the narrow gate. For wide is the gate and broad is the road that leads to destruction, and many enter through it. But small is the gate and narrow the road that leads to life, and only a few find it."** [30]

Everyone can be saved, but only a few will be saved.

I came to believe that God created the heavens and the earth for a specific purpose. He has invited all humans to the wedding banquet He has prepared for his only begotten Son.

"Many are invited, but few are chosen."

Are you one of the chosen guests?

To close this book and open the door to the main hall of the wedding banquet, I will leave you with the most valuable right of a human being.

"Everyone has the right to freedom of thought, conscience and religion. This right includes freedom to change religion or belief and freedom, either alone or in community with others and in public or in private, to manifest religion or belief, in worship, teaching, practice and observance." [31]

---

[30] Matthew 7:13-14
[31] Charter of Fundamental Human Rights

OUR FATHER IN HEAVEN

HALLOWED BE YOUR NAME

YOUR KINGDOM COME

YOUR WILL BE DONE ON EARTH

AS IT IS IN HEAVEN

GIVE US TODAY OUR DAILY BREAD

FORGIVE OUR DEBTS

    AS WE ALSO HAVE FORGIVEN OUR DEBTORS

AND LEAD US NOT INTO TEMPTATION

    BUT DELIVER US FROM THE EVIL ONE

FOR THE KINGDOM THE POWER AND THE

GLORY ARE YOURS NOW AND FOREVER MORE

AMEN

…

www.ingramcontent.com/pod-product-compliance
Lightning Source LLC
Chambersburg PA
CBHW031543210526
45464CB00003B/1127